SADDLE Your HORSE

TRIAL, FAITH, AND TRIUMPH

SADDLE YOUR HORSE

TRIAL, FAITH, AND TRIUMPH

Marian Asamoah-Anim

Saddle Your Horse, Trial, Faith and Triumph

Copyright © 2024 by Marian Asamoah-Anim

ISBN- 13: 979-8-218-52437-1

All rights reserved. Printed in the United States of America. The author guarantees all contents are original and do not infringe upon the legal rights of any other person or work. No part of this book may be used or reproduced in any form whatsoever without written permission from the author.

Unless otherwise stated, all scripture quotations are taken from the Holy Bible, New International Version, NIV, Copyright @ 1997 by Thomas Nelson. Please refuse participation in the pirating or duplication of copyrighted materials, which hurts and violates the rights of the author. Please purchase ONLY authorized copies from legitimate sellers.

First Edition: November 17, 2024
Christian Living
Self-Help
Healthy Living
Women Empowerment

Contact the Author:
office@JesusisLordcrusades.org
www.JesusisLordcrusades.org
www.josephdreampublishing.com

DEDICATION

To

*Clement, my loving husband.
Thank you for selflessly sharing me with the world and for supporting me as I fulfill my calling to serve this generation. Your love and encouragement mean more than words can express.*

To

*Nana Kweku and Kofi (Children),
Words can't fully express how deeply I love you both. Whether near or far, you are always in my heart. You were made for greatness! Keep soaring high!*

To

Mrs. Linda Ampah, my beloved sister who also played the role of mother in my life. Thank you for teaching me how to "Snap out of it to move on." You are the true epitome of the Shunammite woman.

To

Priscilla Boama of Pentecost Women. You are proof of what God can do when we are obedient to His call.

To

Pentecost Women, thank you all for inspiring this book.

FOREWORD

The simple Christian narrative seems to be you sow a seed and you reap a harvest, or you go through a test and you get a testimony then you live happily ever after. If you walk with God long enough you will realize that the Christian walk is not that simple. After sowing and reaping a harvest, your harvest can be attacked or attract attacks and new problems. Your testimony after your test can attract new and more difficult tests and trials. Life happens even when you are walking with God.

In this book, Saddle Your Horse, Evangelist Marian Asamoah-Anim uses the story of the Shunammite woman and her son, as told in 2 Kings 4:18–20, to teach lessons on how the Christian can navigate the complex ups and downs in our walk with God in this world. If you are going through trials and challenges, this is a book you need to read. If you are trying to help others navigate through their issues, this is an excellent resource. Even if you have not experienced any major trials or tests in your walk with God, you need to read this book to prepare yourself for the inevitable.

I like the fact that this book does not end with the chapter captioned "It is WELL" but with the chapter captioned "Hold On! Keep Your Saddle Ready." It is my prayer that this book will equip the reader to be always vigilant and ready for whatever the enemy will throw at us by constantly keeping our saddle ready.

Rev. Dr George Addae-Mintah
Senior Pastor (Agape Life Ministries)

TABLE OF CONTENTS

DEDICATION v

FOREWORD vi

INTRODUCTION 1

CHAPTER ONE: LIFE HAPPENS! 7

CHAPTER TWO: SHHH… SHUT THE DOOR 19

CHAPTER THREE: BREAKING PROTOCOL 31

CHAPTER FOUR: SADDLE, SADDLE, SADDLE!!! 45

CHAPTER FIVE: AT THE MASTER'S FEET 57

CHAPTER SIX: IT IS WELL! 73

CHAPTER SEVEN: HOLD ON! KEEP YOUR SADDLE READY ... 83

CONCLUSION 92

THANK YOU 107

SALVATION PRAYER 108

INTRODUCTION

Life is certainly a journey filled with unexpected twists and turns, moments of highs and lows with bursts of unspeakable joy, and at other times of profound challenges and tragedies, and no one is exempt from this experience. One minute we are enjoying what is called "The Blessings of the Lord" and the next minute, like Job in the Bible, it's BOOM!!!!!! Lights fade, silence emerges, and family and friends abandon you at your lowest moment.

In the midst of challenges, it's common to question ourselves. The questions of self-worth, shame, and sometimes doubt such as, "God, how can this happen to me?" I am a tither, giver, prayer warrior, and, yes, one who is given to fasting. So, why is this happening to me? God, how could you let this happen to me?"

I am certain that everyone reading this book has had their share of unexpected events. While it is painful, life, unfortunately, does not stand still waiting for us to catch up; rather, the days keep moving and the hours keep changing.

Despite all our challenges, one thing is certain and it is the restorative power of God. His power is readily available for all who desire it. Seldom do we get the answers to why we face challenging issues as believers; nor do we understand why bad things happen to good people. Rather, it is how we navigate in those trying times that define the course of our lives and shape our character and relationship with God.

While I might not have the answers to your questions on whether your problem is God's will or not, I would rather encourage you to celebrate the fact that God can turn every sorrow into joy.

> *You have turned for me my mourning into dancing.*
> *You have loosed my sackcloth and clothed me with gladness.*
> **PSALM 30:11 ESV**

There is no question that your situation, present or past, is incredibly painful. God has a perfect solution or lesson even in the trauma of that pain that we often cannot see or understand. In my case; the devastating loss of my mother at age four was painful beyond words. It changed my life and those of my siblings tremendously. My eldest sister had to become our surrogate mother whilst still a child herself. My childhood was full of uncertainties, traumatic, and sometimes even chaotic.

INTRODUCTION

But it was in that time of vulnerability and hopelessness that I was introduced to God who gives us the saddle to ride in His direction of hope and love. I have seen how trying times can easily make you think God has forgotten you, but it is in these moments that we trust God even the most. When you allow Him to work through the pain, He can erase the years of that pain in a manner that becomes almost unexplainable. The joy of the morning has the power to eradicate the sorrows of the night.

As recounted in the Bible, the story of the Shunammite woman and her son offers timeless lessons in transforming challenges into triumphs. It is about the power of unwavering faith, the importance of persistence, the refusal to give in and give up, and the redeeming quality of finding your inner strength in your most challenging moments.

In Saddle Your Horse, we explore the theme of saddling and riding through life's storms to reach our victories. The phrase "saddle your horse" signifies preparation, steady determination, and personal resolution to face whatever lies ahead. Just as a rider must be ready to mount their horse and navigate difficult terrain, we too must be prepared to confront and overcome the obstacles in our paths.

While life may have started well for the rich Shunammite woman as a hospitable hostess to Prophet Elisha, she ended up being beautifully blessed by the unexpected miraculous birth of her son prophesied by him. However, her BOOM moment happened when her son fell ill and died. Instead of succumbing to despair, she saddled her horse—figuratively and literally—in search of Elisha, the Lord's prophet. In pain, yet driven by relentless hope, unbending faith, and her belief in the possibility of a second miracle, she triumphed in the end.

The Shunammite woman's journey is a powerful metaphor for our own lives in Christ as believers. What should we do when faced with seemingly insurmountable challenges? We have two choices: to be defeated by them or to rise above them and seek our victory.

The Shunammite woman's determination, resilience, and faith should serve as a reminder to all of us that even in the darkest moments there is a path to triumph if we are willing to persevere.

Saddle Your Horse delves into different Christian principles while applying both practical and spiritual tools needed to transform our everyday lives. My prayer is that the tools laid out in this book will equip you with the ability to face life's challenges head-on. Saddle your horse and ride through that adversity

INTRODUCTION

knowing that, with faith and perseverance, victory is within your reach. Join me on this reading journey of Saddle Your Horse to find both spiritual inspiration and inner strength in the Shunammite woman's story.

Let her unwavering faith and strength from the Holy Spirit guide you chapter by chapter. May you receive strength as you navigate through your trials and may it lead you to the victories that wait for you on the other side. I see you rising!

E.M.

God is awesome in his sanctuary.
The God of Israel gives power an*d strength to his people.*

PSALM 68:35

SADDLE YOUR HORSE

CHAPTER ONE
LIFE HAPPENS!

Life Happens!

18 The child grew, and one day he went out to his father, who was with the reapers. 19 He said to his father, "My head! My head!" His father told a servant, "Carry him to his mother." 20 After the servant had lifted him up and carried him to his mother, the boy sat on her lap until noon, and then he died.

2 KINGS 4:18–20

LIFE HAPPENS

Life happens! One minute you are enjoying God's promises, the great job, the new house, and your children are off to college, and then the next minute the unexpected happens. You lose your job; your house catches fire, and a child is suddenly sick with an incurable disease! Life, in its own unique and unpredictable manner, has a way of catching us off guard by presenting us with moments of unexpected joy and sudden heartaches. Many times, we forget that these moments, whether fleeting or long-lasting, often hold profound golden life lessons we need for personal and spiritual growth. The narration of the Shunammite woman and her son, as told in 2 Kings 4:18–20, encapsulates degrees of various moments from what started as a normal day in the life of the Shunammite woman, her husband and child but ended as a completely unexpected tragedy with the loss of her son!

Life happens! The unexpected late-night phone call from the police or the death of someone you had just seen the day before uses the Shunammite woman's story to teach us about the changeable nature of life and the powerful lessons we must draw from all of it—the good, bad and ugly side when we are faced with the unimaginable. For some of us who have lived a sheltered life, to experience its harshness might even be more unsettling than it must have been for the Shunammite woman, a high society woman who was not only rich but well-connected and had come to terms with being childless. She had accepted her fate and lived her life without hopes of being a mother. Her faith remained intact despite her situation, what a remarkable woman! While not every woman might want to be a mother, in her case, I believe she did resign herself to the fact that it was not going to ever happen to her.

Then life happened. During one of Prophet Elisha's many ministerial travels, she acted in her usual hostess fashion, tending and caring for the man of God. Prophet Elisha saw beyond her façade and gave a prophetic word that would change her family's life forever. While she showed resistance, she accepted and the following year she gave birth to a handsome son. Life was great until, like every other day, her husband took their son to the field with him and the unexpected happened. To appreciate the full story of the Shunammite woman and even our personal lives, we all as individuals believe that there are things in life, we are working on that we want to see grow.

We want to grow in our employment, businesses, family, and even ministry. We have dreams of our children growing, eager to see what they become as adults. Who they will marry, who our grandchildren will resemble in our families. We have dreams of moving from a one-bedroom apartment to a sprawling ten-square-foot mansion overlooking the Atlantic Ocean. As we age, we also have dreams of retirement, becoming a best-selling author, and being able to travel around the world.

Life is about the joys of growing that sometimes do come with a bit of pain as well. However, growth is a beautiful thing because it speaks to expansion and development; the power to multiply your presence in a place or even industry. The very first experience of growth is seen in the Book of Genesis 1:28 in which God's greatest creation was man, He commanded him to be fruitful and multiply.

> *27 So God created man in His own image; in the image of God, He created him; male and female He created them. 28 Then God blessed them, and God said to them, "Be fruitful and multiply; fill the earth and subdue it; have dominion over the fish of the sea, over the birds of the air, and over every living thing that moves on the earth."*
>
> **GENESIS 1:27–28 NKJV**

It is in the nature of man not only to be fruitful but to multiply what he has deemed fruitful. Companies like Amazon, Google, Microsoft, and a host of Fortune 500 companies are in the constant business of not only being profitable but having multiple chains like McDonald's, Wendy's, or even banks. And we as people are no different and neither was the son of the Shunammite woman. The growth of her son depicts the natural progression of life, its joy, and normalcy, as he grows and falls into that familiar family pattern of daily routine of life.

Often in our own lives, we feel blessed and content; we have a rhythm to life, and our set routines are working out for all of us. Everyone knows their roles and thriving in them. The predictability of life is what gives us a sense of security and stability. Every family and individual strive for security and stability, which is no different for the Shunammite woman's family.

Part of growth is experiencing different things in life and for the child who had grown, it was time for him to go out with his father. Isn't that the beauty of life? One minute your child is in a car seat and then the next minute they are driving their own car! For him, it was time to be with his father in the field. He was in the place of transitioning and often where there is growth there also lies adjustment as well. While he was younger, he probably spent a lot of time with his mother in the house, but when he was all grown up, he could go out to the field with his father, and perhaps learn the ins and outs of the business.

The fact of the matter is that it was like any normal day in which he went to the field with his father and the workers. And in the twinkle of an eye, he seemed to be complaining of a headache. His father took it lightly and assigned his son to one of the servants to take to his mother. And suddenly what started as a regular day out in the field was shattered as his headache only seemed to be worsening by the minute. The normalcy of the day was suddenly interrupted and his father's immediate reaction was to have him carted off to his mother. His cry of pain has great significance and becomes a pivotal turning point in the household.

This often happens in life. What was just a little abdominal discomfort that sent one to a routine medical check-up led to the discovery of stage-four pancreatic cancer. What was an invitation by a business partner in which you thought you were getting a performance bonus that led to a lay-off and another person getting your position. Your excitement at joining a large church could lead to a nationwide scandal. What was a regular day could suddenly turn into a life crisis! His father, though he masks it well, was undoubtedly panicked and afraid and sent his child off to his mother.

His father sending him off to his mother signifies his sense of helplessness. Perhaps he had the self-doubt that he was ill-equipped to help his son at that very moment. For the father at that exact moment, life happened to him. We are often narrow-minded in our moments of challenges, forgetting that others around us are also experiencing the same pain as we do, and maybe even at a greater level—imagine the guilt of his father, the self-loathing, thinking that, possibly, if his son had not come out to the field that day, he would not be in crisis.

The truth is that in times of crisis, we are allowed to feel a sense of momentary helplessness. We are allowed to put some trust in those closest to us without replacing God with them. His father asking the servant to carry him to his mother not only signifies that he believes that the mother has the solution but possibly he was afraid of the situation worsening. Sometimes we do not know how people will react in such fragile life moments. While those who we often run to may offer us the nurturing comfort that we need at that moment, the truth is that the comfort provided won't last when it is an unforeseen emergency.

This father-son moment captures the essence of how life can abruptly change, thrusting us into crises we are unprepared for and yet we muster the courage to face it head-on. In times of crisis, new things are discovered as new paths are sought to find a solution for the raging problem. The servant does as he is instructed, and carries the child to his mother; no words are spoken while sitting on her lap, and at noon he dies. Sometimes words are insufficient to express the type of grief one is experiencing at that time. Words become meaningless during a crisis. Perhaps she had given up as a mother, but whatever might have been the case, her grief was unbearable and unquantifiable to express.

The image of the mother holding her only son until he died is both heartbreaking and powerful. It speaks to the deep bond between mother and child that even in the direst of situations—dying—there is an unspeakable comfort in such a bond. It is a bond that does not need words to express a mother's love. The Shunammite woman's reaction to holding her son close during his final moments displays a mother's act of profound love, compassion, and resignation. As human beings, we hold things or people that we love, and the harder we hold them the more it speaks to the deep love that we have for them.

The mother's action here underscores the helplessness we all feel when life happens, most importantly when we are forced to confront the reality of our limitations. And for many people who are faced with life's bad moments, this is often where they end their chapter. They accept that which or whom they love is over; they tell themselves that this is probably the way God wanted it to be. They resign themselves to fate and shut their hearts to anything good or happy again. Often, we are struck by the finality of a situation, hopeless, and afraid that this is it when it does not have to be.

Life did not happen to the Shunammite woman alone but to her husband, the reapers, the servant, and most certainly her dead son. No matter how bad something might seem, we must resolve to find a solution for a way forward. We must create new memories that grow us as well. The death of her son was an opportunity for growth for her as well. We should never minimize the pain or loss of an individual; the challenge is how to grow from it in order not to be defeated by it. The loss of a child who comes when you have given up on being a mother cannot be compared to a replaceable job loss.

I believe that while she held her dead son in her arms, so many thoughts and memories would have flooded her mind. Memories of joy and pain, thoughts of the future, and perhaps his wedding day. I believe that she might have lost hope as her dead son lies in her arms, I believe that her faith pushed her through the circumstances and moved her into action. No one can tell you how long you should mourn over an incident, but let us be encouraged to find the courage and know that no matter how life happens, we must get up and find a way forward. I can assure you through the Word of God that when the pain is handed over to Jesus, He will turn it around. This I know for sure.

SADDLE YOUR HORSE

CHAPTER TWO
SHHH... SHUT THE DOOR

SHHH... SHUT THE DOOR

21 She went up and laid him on the bed of the man of God, then shut the door and went out.

2 KINGS 4:21

SHHH... SHUT THE DOOR

The words "Shut the door" are mentioned at least thirty-one times throughout the Bible from the gallant actions of Ehud in Judges 3:23 to the widow and her two sons whom creditors were in pursuit of in II Kings 4:4. Shutting the door often signifies a life-altering change or some type of judgment. The Merriam-Webster dictionary has several definitions of shutting down; in the case of losing her son, the definition would be "to confine as if by enclosure" on the prophet's bed.

This single act of shutting the door encapsulates a pivotal moment in the Shunammite woman's life. The death of her son offers profound and life-changing lessons that we must all glean from as Christians. The scene is unimaginable as she carries her son's lifeless but warm body into the room of the prophet and lays him on his bed. Every step for her must have been agonizing, every memory debilitating, yet she lays him in place and shuts the door.

This act of closing the door is symbolic and instructive, representing her decision to focus on faith and act without distraction. She saw no need for commotion or drama. She did not cry or wail. This sudden affliction called for guarding one's lips. It might seem like she wanted to conceal his death until she had the time to process what had happened, or perhaps she knew exactly what she wanted to do. The Shunammite woman might have concluded that not every issue needs noise and not every journey needs a crowd.

In our lives, we often face moments of intense despair and confusion. The natural reaction is for us to dwell on the pain, but the Shunammite woman's actions teach us the importance of creating a space for faith and hope. By shutting the door, she closes off the noise of doubt and despair. She created a private, sacred space where she could focus on seeking divine intervention. As Christians, and especially people of faith, when faced with crises, we should all be encouraged to follow her example.

Sometimes we must shut the door deliberately, stepping away from the very source of our distress and focusing on the solutions. It means creating an environment where we can think clearly, pray fervently, and strategically plan our next steps without being overwhelmed by negativity. Just as when Jesus entered the house of the synagogue leader whose daughter had died in Mark 5:38–40; Jesus sent everyone out of the room so He could be alone with the little girl.

SHHH... SHUT THE DOOR

> *38 Then He came to the house of the ruler of the synagogue and saw [g]a tumult and those who wept and wailed loudly. 39 When He came in, He said to them, "Why make this commotion and weep? The child is not dead but sleeping." 40 And they ridiculed Him. But when He had put them all outside, He took the father and the mother of the child, and those who were with Him, and entered where the child was lying.*
>
> **MARK 5:38–40**

Sometimes you just need to shut the door to hear clearly what God has in mind for that situation. You must weigh your words carefully in order not to say anything contrary to what God has proposed. There is time for everything! Not all issues are handled the same way. Wisdom is needed for the execution of knowledge received. Your actions during a crisis are very important as it sets the tone for the outcome. I have learned to keep my mouth shut about most situations. Allow God to work with you privately before sharing it.

The Shunammite woman's reaction to her son's death is a perfect example of a person who knows their God and is secure in their identity. When our confidence lies in God, situations cannot drown us, and this was the case for the Shunammite woman. She was not ready to make noise, no call on her neighbors or the ambulance. She had faith and believed in God.

The Shunammite woman placed her son on Elisha's bed, this was purely an act of faith. She could have laid the child on any other bed in the house, so why this particular one? This is what I perceived as I meditated on this verse. We must be mindful of where we choose to lay our issues. She knew the prophet was a man of God and carried God's presence; therefore, there ought to be a residue of that presence in his room. That was a point of contact for her.

She decided to place her problem in the presence of God, symbolically laying her burden in the presence of the one who could help her. It was not about Elisha; it was about the God of Elisha.

She connected her son at once to an anointing that broke yokes and was able to bring the dead back to life the moment she laid his corpse on the prophet's bed in the upper room. It is the same principle with which the disciples' lives were transformed by the Holy Spirit in the upper room in Acts 1:12-13.

SHHH... SHUT THE DOOR

> *12 Then they returned to Jerusalem from the mount called Olivet, which is near Jerusalem, a Sabbath day's journey. 13 And when they had entered, they went up into the upper room where they were staying: Peter, James, John, and Andrew; Philip and Thomas; Bartholomew and Matthew; James the son of Alphaeus and Simon the Zealot; and Judas the son of James. 14 These all continued with one [d]accord in prayer [e]and supplication, with the women and Mary the mother of Jesus, and with His brothers.*
>
> ACTS 1:12–13

The upper room holds great significance as it pertains to the Christian faith walk. It is the place of divine encounter as we will find out in subsequent chapters of this book. In the days of the Acts of the Apostles, the upper room was the birthplace of the Christian Church, the descending of the Holy Spirit, and the launching of the apostolic ministry globally.

The Upper Room is where Jesus held His Last Supper, introducing us to the profound power of Communion. It is in the Upper Room where we meet Jesus—a place where divinity meets humanity and the miraculous unfolds. Similarly, when the Shunammite woman laid her son on the prophet's bed, this symbolic gesture was like placing him at the altar of the Most High. By doing so, she was offering her son as a sacrifice to God, trusting Him for spiritual restoration.

We must learn from her actions. When faced with seemingly insurmountable problems, we too should lay them at altar of the Most High God. This means praying earnestly, seeking His guidance, and trusting in His power to provide solutions. By surrendering our challenges to Him, we acknowledge His sovereignty—recognizing that some battles are beyond our control and require divine intervention.

When the Shunammite woman laid her son on the prophet's bed, her actions signified three important steps we as Christians must take when we commit our struggles to God.

- Positioning – The Shunammite woman positioned her son properly. In our deepest and darkest times, we must realize that positioning ourselves and the things that we love is vital. When we are positioned properly, God can do supernatural things in our lives.
- Prepared – Unpreparedness for your miracle can be considered a tragedy. If we are expecting God to raise the

dead, we must be prepared for the miracle. The five foolish virgins were unprepared for the bridegroom and lost out in the end. Let us remain prepared even in times of difficulty.

- Establish – Make up your mind once and for all that this is it. We must settle what we want in our minds and remain steadfast. The Shunammite woman's resolve was settled and she was committed.

Things must happen spiritually before they can manifest physically and, as spiritual people, we must all learn how to handle things from a spiritual perspective first and foremost. The Shunammite woman refused to accept the death of her only son and turned a tragedy around by applying spiritual principles to a physical situation. This prophetic action was considered a spiritual transaction. On completion, it would provoke a physical manifestation.

By laying her son on the prophet's bed, she was stating that she only viewed him as sleeping and not dead. She did not make any noise so as not to affect the will of God but kept her mouth shut. There is sometimes power in the place of solitude. By shutting the door and laying her son on the bed of the prophet, the Shunammite woman created a moment of solitude. A quiet place where she could gather her thoughts, pray, and strategize what her next steps would be. Solitude in a time of crisis can be a powerful tool when we sometimes do not see a way out.

In the contemporary times that we live in, solitude can be difficult to come by; bombarded by work, social media, and the everyday demands of life, the art of quietness has been lost to many. Yet, if we can shut the door and make time for both our mental and spiritual well-being, we can live more meaningful and healthier lives. Learning how to shut the door both literally and figuratively is an art form needed to create wholesome places to think, pray, and reflect.

Laying her son on the bed of the prophet, the Shunammite woman was not only laying her son symbolically upon the altar of God, but she was returning to the foundation of her faith. There is something about tragedy that propels us to a crossroads in life. It either pushes us closer to God or away from Him. Closer to His unfailing love or away into the destruction of Satan. Tragedy exposes not only our faith but the foundation on which it is built.

The Bible speaks about foundations numerous times and how challenges will test our foundation. A man built a house upon sand and when the storm came, it washed it away unlike the man who built his upon the rock. He was able to withstand the storm and the flood (Luke 6:49). Job loved the Lord and yet he was struck with multiple tragedies from which he recovered, even though Satan had requested from God to test his foundation.

The Shunammite woman returned to the ABC of her faith walk. She leaned on the foundational knowledge of God and His promises. She laid everything at the altar of God, went up into Elisha's room, and then went out of it. She did not take time to pause or weep, there was no time for that. She decided that she wanted to get into action and that is what she did.

I believe that sometimes in life, when there is deep pain, words become insufficient and faith must kick in along with resolve. I want to let you know that it is time to lay that precious burden on the altar of the Most High God and move toward the execution stage of your faith. We had no idea what the Shunammite woman had planned, but we knew that she was going to act after she shut the door. Sometimes we also do not know what we are going to do either, but we know that decisive action is the only solution.

This silent action by the Shunammite woman speaks to the importance of acting in the face of adversity. She did not spend a single moment lamenting (how would that have changed anything?). For many of us, it is so easy to allow the pain, fear, and disappointment of a tragedy to paralyze us into inactivity. How many times have we all chosen to lie down depressed over a loss or situation? But we cannot remain immobilized by fear. We have to take the steps needed to address our problems even when the outcome is unclear and we don't have all the answers. Through the Word of God, we have what it takes to shut the door and move forward! Your presence matters, you are needed and your story will be a blessing to many generations. God is ready to partner with you. I encourage you to take a moment and cry out to him right now. "Lord, help me."

CHAPTER THREE
BREAKING PROTOCOL

Breaking Protocol

22 She called her husband and said, "Please send me one of the servants and a donkey so I can go to the man of God quickly and return." 23 "Why go to him today?" he asked. "It's not the New Moon or the Sabbath." "That's all right," she said.

2 KINGS 4:22–23

BREAKING PROTOCOL

When I think of women who exemplify courage in the Bible, there are a few women who top the list such as Queen Esther, Deborah, and the valiant Shunammite woman. She represents a powerful example of a married woman who had the tenacity to break both societal and religious protocol to achieve the greater good. When her son died, she refused to conform to the expected customs of her time.

Instead, she took decisive and unconventional steps to seek God with the help of the man of God, Elisha. There will be instances in our lives when we will have to decide if we will break protocol to attain the miraculous. Protocol refers to the official way, norms, or rules that govern one's actions or behavior. In layman's terms, it means doing something in a manner that is expected of one. Often, we are expected to maintain a certain type of protocol whether in our workplace, place of worship, or in public.

There will be times when we will need to break protocol to get what we need as long as it's not illegal or harming anyone. In moments like this, I think of the woman with the issue of blood in Mark 5:25–34. Just like the women before her, she broke protocol to receive her miracle! How many times have you denied yourself an opportunity because you were afraid to break protocol? And what was the ultimate cost to you? What would have been your reward if you had done so?

We must have the courage that nothing will stop us from receiving what God has promised us. Just like the woman with the issue of blood, she was determined that no manmade protocol would prevent her from getting her miracle! The actions of the Shunammite woman provide several applicable life lessons one can draw from in the modern-day context for us to attain all that God has for us.

The first thing about breaking protocol is that you know the consequences of doing so. It is not something done lightly or recklessly. It is a position that, once taken, you accept the cost that follows by taking such a drastic decision. It requires both courage and resolve, often made without a backup plan involved.

During ancient times in Israel, societal and religious protocols were strictly adhered to, governing everyday facets of daily living. Women especially had clearly defined roles and the expectation was that they stayed within them. The significance of the Shunammite woman's actions was mind-blowing as she defied both societal and religiously established norms!

Equipped with quiet resolve and an unwavering mindset, the second thing the Shunammite woman did out of the norm was to request the use of their vehicle (aka donkey) and a servant to see the man of God. She told her husband it would be a quick visit with prophet Elisha.

The new moon and the Sabbath were times reserved for religious observance and seeking prophetic counsel, so her request was out of the norm, particularly because they often housed him so her husband couldn't understand her urgency to see the man of God. One of the greatest dangers a person faces in breaking protocol is trying to explain your level of urgency to someone else. No man or woman in the Bible who broke protocol ever took the time to explain their decisions to others. And just like those before her, the Shunammite woman's insistence on seeing Elisha despite her husband's questioning reveals her determination, faith, and resolve.

She refused to explain her plight to anyone including her husband! Nothing could stop her from receiving her miracle. It was between her and her God. The danger of explaining opens the door for people to dissuade you from your decision. How many times have you resolved to take a particular action and shared it with others and years later regretted your indecision or decision?

The third life lesson the Shunammite woman provides is the power to move immediately. Her immediate reaction after the death of her son was to seek out Elisha, who had promised her the child. She broke from the protocol of mourning her son and the traditional rites of death. By breaking this practice, she prioritized her faith and the urgency of her need over manmade customs.

In some instances, breaking up customs may lead to temporary or permanent change. In today's world, we have seen how different cultures have changed the way they practice the rites of death. For some, they use it as a celebration of life; for others, it's a time of loss and sober reflection. For the Shunammite woman, it was an opportunity not to wallow in depression but to press forward for a solution.

The Shunammite woman's demonstration of transcending religious boundaries is reminiscent of the ministry of Jesus Christ who often did miracles outside of the prescribed religious timetable. Her action mirrored that of Jesus Christ especially when her husband asked, "Why go to him today? It's not the new moon or the Sabbath," which highlights the expectation that religious matters should be addressed on specific days.

She broke the norm by interpreting her need to exceed customary boundaries. This is something that Jesus often did, breaking religious systems to address the needs of His people. Her faith in God's power and Elisha's prophetic authority drove her to act immediately.

One of the greatest gifts of the Shunammite woman's legacy is the power of taking the initiative! She did not wait for an "appropriate" time to seek help or wait for someone else to solve her problem. She recognized the importance of acting in the moment, teaching the lesson that we must break out of our comfort zones and challenge established norms to achieve our goals. There are so many Christians who live by the principle "I am waiting on the Lord" when the Bible clearly states, "Faith without works is dead." (James 2:18–20)

> *18 But someone will say, "You have faith, and I have works." Show me your faith without your works, and I will show you my faith by [b]my works. 19 You believe that there is one God. You do well. Even the demons believe—and tremble! 20 But do you want to know, O foolish man, that faith without works is dead.*
>
> **JAMES 2:18–20**

I have often felt that this has become a crutch for many Christians—to wait on the sidelines for God to show up while they do nothing, often allowing Satan to steal, kill, and destroy, leading to frustration and disappointment instead of hope for significant change. Waiting for the perfect time or following conventional paths may not always bring the solutions we need. The Shunammite woman's initiative demonstrates that faith, combined with decisive action, can lead to miraculous outcomes.

By breaking protocol, the Shunammite woman also defied societal expectations in a time when women were expected to be passive in matters of religious significance—she was not! Just like the Shunammite woman, the modern-day Christian woman should learn that docile women do not impact the Kingdom! The Shunammite woman did not let Israel's religious customs hinder her faith. Instead, she took charge of the situation and displayed strength and resilience that rose above the confinement of her societal role.

Sadly, this aspect of the Shunammite woman's story still rings particularly true even in today's society and Church. The relevancy and irony of her story cannot be ignored as women and men alike often face societal pressures, prejudices, and expectations that limit their potential. How many people do you know who would break from the protocol of their church or societal routine in fear of rejection or judgment? We must let the Shunammite example of exemplary courage inspire us to rise above these limitations and pursue our goals with determination and faith, regardless of societal and religious norms.

"Speech is silver while silence is golden" is believed to have originated out of ancient Egypt and was made popular by poet Thomas Carlyle in 1831. This quote is evident in the Shunammite woman's short conversation with her husband who is blissfully unaware of the death of their son. In all his questioning and skepticism, she simply responded, "That's all right." Her brevity speaks volumes about her resolve.

She breaks yet another sacred protocol in which many people like to believe that every single action should be discussed between spouses. However, sometimes breaking protocol is not about seeking permission or validation but rather informing your loved one of your decisions.

Determination is a crucial trait in breaking protocol, requiring a steadfast commitment to our goals and a willingness to face criticism or doubt afterward. The Shunammite woman's unwavering determination serves as a reminder that achieving extraordinary results often requires extraordinary resolve on our part.

Behind every broken protocol, there is a motive that must be explored to understand the decision made behind breaking that protocol. And for the Shunammite woman, at the very heart of her decision was the desperation of a mother seeking divine intervention for her dead son. Every time protocol has been broken in certain parts of the world, it has been discovered that the motive behind it, which was often at the center of that decision, was desperation.

The Shunammite woman was no different. She knew that Elisha, *as a true man of God*, held the key to her son's restoration. Her actions were not just about defying norms but seeking God's higher power to address her crisis. To experience divine intervention in our lives means stepping outside of conventional methods to do so. It is often uncomfortable, and unfamiliar but also involves trusting in God's ability and being willing to take bold steps of faith. The Shunammite woman's story teaches us that breaking protocol can be a powerful way to invite God's miraculous intervention into our circumstances.

Breaking protocol allows us to find the power to challenge the status quo and opens the door to new and endless possibilities. Most importantly, it can inspire others to take bold actions in their own lives and about decisions that they have often questioned or were discouraged to make. In today's world, breaking protocol can take many forms from challenging traditional careers and roles to exploring unconventional career paths involving risk-taking or workplace advocacy. This also includes advocacy for marginalized groups.

Challenging unjust policies and working toward equality often requires courage and determination. For many of us, breaking protocol on a personal level means stepping out in faith to take on bold actions in the pursuit of our dreams, trusting in divine guidance along the way. As a woman, taking bold steps to organize gospel crusades not only breaks the norms but also challenges societal expectations.

Moving against the grain of traditional expectations is often a difficult path but moving in the direction God leads us is rarely easy. We must follow the voice of God and act accordingly, even when it feels like we are defying what the world expects of us. However, it is important to remember that we do not do this in disrespect, but rather in obedience to God's calling, trusting that His ways are higher than ours.

Through resilience, faith, and bold action, we show that we can stand firm, even when the journey is tough. When we step out in faith, we are not only pursuing our personal goals but also challenging the systems that hold back progress, ultimately working towards a greater sense of justice and equality.

The Shunammite woman's ability to break protocol started the very moment she shut the door and turned despair into determination, choosing faith over depression. This once-passive woman found the strength to take the initiative in the direction of her miracle. In the end, she turns a tragic situation into a testimony of God's power.

BREAKING PROTOCOL

As we navigate our own lives, we should be inspired by the Shunammite woman's example of breaking protocol, understanding the power of divine intervention, and taking decisive steps that align with our faith and goals. By doing so, we open ourselves to the possibility of extraordinary outcomes and the fulfillment of our greatest potential. You can do it!

SADDLE YOUR HORSE

CHAPTER FOUR
SADDLE, SADDLE, SADDLE!!!

Saddle, Saddle, Saddle!!!

24 She saddled the donkey and said to her servant, "Lead on; don't slow down for me unless I tell you."

2 KINGS 4:24

SADDLE, SADDLE, SADDLE!!!

No sooner does the Shunammite tell her husband of her need to see Prophet Elisha than she purposefully saddles her horse, driven by faith and urgency.

This means more than simply the physical process of preparation for a journey; it represents the intentional and resolute mindset required to confront problems head-on. I find it very interesting that she saddles her donkey, not her servant or her husband. She does it alone while commanding her servant to take the lead. She orders him to move with the same urgency Jehu moved, former commander turned king!

Why saddle your horse? Saddling one's horse allows for the equal distribution of the rider's weight across the back of the horse. This ensures minimal pressure on the rider while avoiding potential injuries. The Shunammite woman who saddled her horse purposefully was in search of not only an answer from Elisha but also a solution as well. Everyone wants answers, but where we go for those answers matters immensely. Many people have been wounded because they had placed their entire hope and trust in man more than in God.

Satan, the enemy of our life, has a plethora of tactics at his disposal to divert us from our actual mission, but we cannot let him triumph if we understand that our answers lie within God through Jesus Christ our Lord. Why beat around the bush when we have received a free access pass to the Presence of God through the death of Jesus Christ? We have been given the grace and the permission to freely walk into the presence of our Father to obtain assistance in a time of need.

> *"Let us therefore come boldly to the throne of grace, that we may obtain mercy and find grace to help in time of need."*
> **HEBREWS 4:16**

The Shunammite woman was in great need and it started with her saddling her horse with razor-like focus with full reliance on God who has all the answers. Every Christian should learn to saddle their horse purposefully, doing so with a clear goal in mind. Our focus should be sharply aligned with our actions along with our objectives! It takes this type of clarity to help us navigate through life's distractions and obstacles, keeping us on the path toward the destination. The Shunammite woman's focus was on reaching Elisha, believing that he could help her son. Her unwavering focus propelled her forward, undeterred by the urgency of her situation.

SADDLE, SADDLE, SADDLE!!!

The saddle for the Shunammite woman holds spiritual significance as well, speaking to the fact that there are certain life journeys we must face alone. Just like Jesus started with twelve disciples, then three, down to one named Peter. From the Garden to the Cross, Jesus must have had an internal conflict, but He had already accepted his fate and was willing to pay the cost during His crucifixion. I believe it was no different for the Shunammite woman, bold and full of faith at home but as she rode towards the prophet she must have suffered moments of self-doubt. But she had already saddled her donkey!

"Saddling the donkey" is a metaphor for preparation and readiness. It signifies the moment when one decides to act and move forward, regardless of the obstacles ahead. In the context of the Shunammite woman's story, it symbolizes her readiness to seek divine intervention and her refusal to accept defeat. There are similarities between the Shunammite woman's journey and that of Jesus to the Cross. Just like Jesus Christ, the Shunammite woman prepared before she embarked on her trip. While saddling her donkey was a practical step, it also represented her mental frame of mind along with her spiritual readiness to face whatever lay ahead.

Saddling purposefully teaches us how to seek God for ourselves, keeping our gaze fixed on Him throughout our journey. We cannot succeed without the Word of God as a reference point; otherwise, we will be tossed by every wave of doctrine. We must be intentional about moving in the direction of our destination, preparing mentally, emotionally, and physically for the challenges ahead. Our emotions must be in check to maintain our focus. Every action that we take speaks to our mental capacity along with our spiritual readiness. Riding is no easy task when life and death lie in the balance!

It proves the point—what gives us all the determination to mount our donkeys in the face of adversity is an intimate knowledge of God in whom we delight. The Shunammite woman had unshakable faith and confidence in God's power and His promises! She was confident that the God who had given her a child would resurrect her son back to life. Her strength stemmed from her intimate personal relationship with God and earlier experiences with His faithfulness. She had a reference point.

She had already seen God's amazing power at work in her life, which strengthened her to act decisively even in the face of immense grief and tragedy. Can you take a moment and remember how God brought you through a tough situation? Let that be a reference point for you. If He did it before; He will do it again!

The Shunammite woman's readiness to act immediately is demonstrated by her saddling the donkey herself. She showed no hesitation or procrastination; she acted swiftly to address her crisis. There was a sense of readiness in her urgency, it was palpable in the way she commanded her servant. She emphasized three areas of importance:

Lead On:

This is significant because while she was in charge, she needed her servant to prepare the way for her and guide her in the direction of the prophet.

Don't Slow Down For Me:

The sense of urgency was so great that she was willing to risk her life and safety to get to the prophet. How was she to tell him to slow down if he was ahead of her? Was she going to resort to a hand signal? Her urgency was intense, revealing her single-minded focus on reaching Elisha as quickly as possible. We must imbibe this same sense of urgency as Christians in times of crisis or regarding important tasks in our lives.

Unless I Tell You:

When faced with a critical situation, the Shunammite woman did not waste any time and her instructions were clear. In critical moments, there is no room for mistakes or missteps. Instructions must be clear, precise, and executed flawlessly. She clearly communicated her goals and expectations. Her quick, decisive actions demonstrated her razor-sharp focus and determination, which are the traits we need in a time of monumental crisis. There can be no guesswork or room for mistakes.

Instead of giving way to despair, she chose confidence in God's sovereignty and goodness. This inner belief gave her the confidence to ride her donkey and set out on a long journey to find prophet Elisha, trusting that God would use His servant to perform another miracle. The Shunammite woman's journey to locate Prophet Elisha was no easy task, whether you look at it physically, psychologically, or socially.

According to certain Biblical scholars, it is believed that the journey of the Shunammite woman from Shunem to where prophet Elisha was in Mt. Carmel took a minimum of six hours! This means that she would have arrived to meet the prophet in the evening since her son died at noon! While Gehazi, Elisha's servant, ran ahead of them, it would take the old prophet, the woman, and her servant another six hours to return to Shunem. What this means is that Elisha did not see the dead boy until the next day. This means that the Shunammite woman rode for twelve hours. This means that she rode all day and all night!

Secondly, from a societal point of view, the Shunammite woman crashed the societal barriers that ancient Israel had placed upon their women. By taking control of her situation and seeking Prophet Elisha, she destroyed these societal norms. Along with this fact, she also annihilated what the behavior of a "socialite" should be. Firstly, she took control; secondly, she redefined the actions of a socialite; thirdly she rode all day and at night to meet the prophet without the proper escort of her husband! Crises will make you do things differently without thinking of your reputation or status!

The psychological barriers that the Shunammite woman shattered remain remarkable to this very day. The truth is that the grief and despair at losing her only son should have paralyzed her; but instead, it motivated her. She pushed through everything she felt and found the strength to act!

This third and final act by the Shunammite woman speaks to the power of overcoming immense obstacles to achieve our goals.

Her story highlights how faith can empower us to persevere even when things appear bleak and dark. Her strong faith in a loving and powerful God fuels her determination to persevere, take the necessary actions, and remain optimistic in the face of adversity.

This type of faith broadens our vision, helps us to see beyond the current crisis, and believes in God's bigger plan and ability to bring about restoration and healing.

Faith played a central role in the Shunammite woman's journey. Her faith in God and Elisha's prophetic abilities gave her the strength to saddle the donkey and embark on a twelve-hour journey, serving as a powerful lesson for us today. Her faith was demonstrated by her stepping out and taking bold steps.

The Shunammite woman's actions to seek out Elisha showed that she trusted in God's plan and timing even when faced with insurmountable challenges. She purposefully showed that women too can lead in times of crisis. She was so effective that everyone she met was on board; she inspired all. Her journey to find Elisha required persistence and resilience. It was her sheer determination to keep going that speaks to the strength of her character. She never gave up!

SADDLE, SADDLE, SADDLE!!!

For us modern-day Christians we must learn to saddle up in today's world gleaning inspiration from the principles of the Shunammite woman's story. The act of "saddling up" and taking decisive action is crucial for every Christian when faced with challenges that require us to take bold steps outside of our comfort zones. We must learn to prepare and act with a sense of urgency and persist in the face of great adversity if we are to build our legacy! We must be willing to take the initiative, lead with purpose, and break barriers that hold us captive to achieve our goals.

I want to leave you with seven action steps to ponder as this chapter closes and they are as follows:

1. Choose to saddle your donkey during life's heavy storms.
2. Keep moving forward when all hope looks like it might be gone.
3. Stay in the Word of God to be continually prepared for life's unexpected challenges.
4. Believe that you are stronger than you know.
5. Take decisive actions and move with urgency even when you do not feel like you want to.
6. Decide today to outride the storm of your life through prayer even if it takes you hours, days, or months to do so.

SADDLE YOUR HORSE

Saddling purposefully is about aligning your actions with your faith and purpose. This means seeking God first while trusting in His guidance and maintaining a clear focus on our goals. By doing so, we equip ourselves to face any challenge with confidence, knowing that God is our ultimate source of help and strength. As we pilot our life journeys, let us embrace the call to action. Let us "saddle, saddle, saddle" and move forward with faith, urgency, and determination, trusting that God will guide us and provide the strength we need to overcome any obstacle.

Chapter Five
At The Master's Feet

At the Master's Feet

And she answered, "It is well." 27 Now when she came to the man of God at the hill, she caught him by the feet, but Gehazi came near to push her away. But the man of God said, "Let her alone; for her soul is in deep distress, and the Lord has hidden it from me, and has not told me."

2 KINGS 4:25–26

The Shunammite woman takes an emotional, spiritual, and intentional journey of faith in her search for Prophet Elisha. Her story provides a profound example of taking purposeful action in the face of a crisis. Her decision to travel such a distance risking her life and reputation to seek out Elisha, the man of God, is a powerful testament to her intentionality, faith, and determination. The truth is that intentionality is the bedrock of purposeful living and the Shunammite woman's decision to saddle her horse was not a spur-of-the-moment reaction.

It was a deliberate and calculated move on her part as she knew exactly what she wanted and needed to do. The power of intentionality should govern our everyday lives, especially during the critical times in which we have to make last-minute decisions that are life-changing. The Shunammite woman not only knew what she needed to do but took the necessary steps to achieve her goal. Every decision she made was deliberate, from saddling her horse to riding for six hours to Elisha; it demonstrated her clear understanding of where her help could come from. It is not enough to talk about what we want in life; we must follow through with intentional decisions as well.

The Shunammite woman's actions were both purposeful and faith-based. Her action to saddle her horse was purposeful, but her journey was underpinned by her faith. We must actively discern where purpose ends and where faith begins in our lives. She believed in Elisha's power as a man of God and trusted that he could help her. Her faith translated into purposeful actions, illustrating the profound connection between belief and behavior. Faith is not just sitting and waiting for God to do something about your situation! The Shunammite woman's faith wasn't passive but active, propelling her into action; she refused to wait for help to come to her but actively went after it.

If we desire the supernatural then we must demonstrate our faith by taking bold steps. And we must move with a sense of urgency understanding that the timing is everything. The Shunammite woman was on a critical mission, it showed in everything she did after the death of her son from saddling her horse to instructing her servant to drive fast. Jehu would replicate her same drive in 2 Kings 9:20 and again in 2 Kings 10:16

> *17 Now a watchman stood on the tower in Jezreel, and he saw the company of Jehu as he came, and said, "I see a company of men." And Joram said, "Get a horseman and send him to meet them, and let him say, 'Is it peace?'" 18 So the horseman went to meet him, and said, "Thus says the king: 'Is it peace?'" And Jehu said, "What have you to do with peace? Turn around and follow me." 20 So the watchman reported, saying, "He went up to them and is not coming back; and the driving is like the driving of Jehu the son of Nimshi, for he drives furiously!"*
>
> 2 KINGS 9:17–18, 20

Commander turned King Jehu replicated the Shunammite woman's drive, which happened five chapters earlier; he rode with intention, deliberation, and planned execution. Jehu rode so furiously that from the palace's distance, he resembled a madman! Imagine driving in such a way that people from a distance could tell that you were riding with divine purpose! Jehu would not stop taking bold steps as well. In the very next chapter, he does not slow down but continues, even inviting Jehonadab, the son of Rechab, on his legendary quest to take down the house of Ahab.

> *15 Now when he departed from there, he met Jehonadab the son of Rechab, coming to meet him; and he greeted him and said to him, "Is your heart right, as my heart is toward your heart?" And Jehonadab answered, "It is." Jehu said, "If it is, give me your hand." So, he gave him his hand, and he took him up to him into the chariot. 16 Then he said, "Come with me, and see my zeal for the Lord." So, they had him ride in his chariot. 17 And when he came to Samaria, he killed all who remained to Ahab in Samaria, till he had destroyed them, according to the word of the Lord which He spoke to Elijah.*
>
> **2 KINGS 10:15–17**

Jehu and the Shunammite woman both understood the "assignments" and both performed them relentlessly. Jehu could have sat on his laurels waiting to be made king, but the assignment given to wipe out the household of Ahab was clear to him and he executed it as God intended. The Shunammite woman, on the other hand, had no prophet to secretly anoint her; nor did she have a host of supporters, but both moved with a sense of urgency and purpose. Both demonstrated the importance of timely action in achieving their goals and we must also move just as swiftly in our lives, especially in critical times.

The Shunammite woman's sense of urgency coupled with her focused determination not only allowed her to communicate her goals and expectations effectively but also prepared her for overcoming the obstacles she would have to face in her journey to Mount Carmel. And here is where many Christians give up, on their way to their Mount Carmel. There are many times when we have great intentions; we tell the whole world we are ready to fight our Goliath and we have faith until we meet a major obstacle and then we begin to buckle like a wall of dominoes.

Dear reader, every journey to our Mount Carmel will be met with unforeseen challenges. However, we have the power to overcome them just like the Shunammite woman who through determination and purposefulness overcame all of hers. It is called the power of resilience in the face of unexpected obstacles. Some of the challenges that the Shunammite woman faced were physical challenges as it was a very physical journey to Mount Carmel; it would have been strenuous, but her determination kept her going. "With God all things are possible."

Traveling by donkey over rough terrain for a long distance would be exhausting, especially for someone dealing with emotional distress. The physical exhaustion and the strain of the journey could have hindered her ability to continue as she had never traveled that type of distance in her life. And certainly, it would not have been under such extreme conditions for a total of twelve hours. But she did, without caring about her body, which was not trained for such a long journey.

The emotional challenge and burden of her son's death must have overwhelmed her, but she focuses on the task at hand, thus helping her navigate this emotional turmoil in her life. Her emotional state could have sapped her energy and resolve, making it harder to focus and persevere in the journey. The opposition and questioning that she got from her husband and perhaps people along the way could have deterred her, but she refused to second-guess herself or her mission.

Travel safety was something to be considered, especially when traveling alone with a servant in a rural area. While they might have started in the afternoon, the potential for danger increased as they had to ride throughout the night, which posed significant risks. They could have become victims of bandits, wild animals, and harsh terrain. Of all which could threaten her safety, physical danger would have been a major concern. It requires courage and determination to proceed, which she found and pressed forward.

Religious and cultural challenges must have been very evident as this trip would require a change of mindset, especially as she was approaching a prophet alone as a married woman! This involved her crossing significant religious and cultural barriers as it was unusual for a woman to take such initiative. She had to overcome internal and external barriers related to cultural and religious expectations. This includes both societal and gender as well, especially the societal norms and gender roles that restricted the actions of women and their movement.

Undertaking such a journey without her husband's direct support or a clear societal mandate would have been frowned upon. Such societal pressure would have discouraged her or led to criticism about her from society and her peers. Her actions could have led to social isolation by her stepping out of the typical roles and expectations for women of her time. Her actions could have ultimately led to a lack of support from her community and even her immediate family.

Keeping her faith alive must have been a supernatural challenge in itself! Her journey required not only physical strength but immense spiritual strength. Trying to maintain her faith in the possibility of a miracle was crucial, yet it must have been constantly challenged by her circumstances and lack of support. And, finally, the logistical challenges she must have faced along the road, the practical aspects that it takes to prepare for a long journey, which she did not have the time to plan for. This would include things like enough food, unexpected weather conditions, and the handling of any unexpected events on the road, which would have been complex and taxing. Logistics could have delayed her journey or forced her to turn back before reaching her destination.

The challenges the Shunammite woman faced on her way to Mount Carmel must have been daunting, but she remained persistent and unwavering in her resolve. One must admire her steadfastness in pursuing her goal to see the prophet. Never for once did she give up or complain despite the potential difficulties of the journey to reach the man of God. We must learn that persistence is often the key to overcoming obstacles and achieving success. There is value in the relentless pursuit of our goals in the face of adversity.

The Shunammite woman arrives at the location of Elisha. From a distance, just like Jehu, the man of God recognizes the silhouette of the Shunammite woman and sends Gehazi to welcome and greet her. His servant Gehazi, whose name happens to mean "depressed or diminished vision," is indeed having such a moment. As he greets her, her response contradicts her situation. Her response holds a lot of meaning as she doesn't show the urgency of why she was there.

I often believe that it wasn't just a matter of faith in God's plan for her dead son but that perhaps she recognized that Gehazi could not help her situation. The Shunammite woman's calm exterior conceals the storm within her heart. It is almost as though one is having an out-of-body experience. Her response teaches us that maintaining a composed demeanor in the face of adversity can be a powerful expression of trust in God's sovereignty. Sometimes words are not enough to express what is going on within us.

And upon reaching Elisha, the Shunammite woman falls at his feet. I believe this was not only an act of humility and desperation, but I also believe it was the weight of all she had been carrying and she finally laid them down before the prophet. God has commanded us in Matthew 11:28 that if we have a burden, we should come to Him for rest.

> *"Are you tired? Worn out? Burned out on religion? Come to me. Get away from me and you'll recover your life. I'll show you how to take a real rest. Walk with me and work with me—watch how I do it. Learn the unforced rhythms of grace. I won't lay anything heavy or ill-fitting on you. Keep company with me and you'll learn to live freely and lightly."*
>
> **MATTHEW 11:28 (MSG)**

It was not just a matter of her recognition of Elisha's role as a conduit of God's power; it was at the Master's feet where we often find our deepest prayers answered. This posture of humility is about surrendering our burdens to God, acknowledging that true help and solace come from Him and Him alone. Falling at the Master's feet has so many biblical implications and blessings that stem from the fact that when we take on that posture, God will do the supernatural in our lives.

Kneeling at the Master's feet is a sign of humility and submission; for the Shunammite woman, it was her single act of display of desperation and vulnerability—two attributes she had been unable to demonstrate to her husband, her servant, or even Gehazi. We need to be kinder to one another as we often do not know the struggles of the people around us. Some just have a way of holding it all in. The Shunammite woman was desperate yet humble at the same time. Her posture signifies her recognition of Elisha's connection to God and her submission to divine authority. Total submission allows God to work miracles in our lives.

Falling at the Master's feet isn't just a sign of humility and submission but also a sign of seeking mercy and forgiveness. In Luke 7:37–38, a woman with an alabaster box anoints Jesus' feet with her tears and wipes them with her hair. This woman was considered a sinner, yet her act of humility and repentance reflected her deep remorse and desire for forgiveness. Jesus acknowledges her faith and forgives her sins. Throughout the Bible, there are instances in which falling at the Master's feet provided invaluable lessons such as the discipleship of Mary or the worship of the man healed from demons in Luke 8:35.

For the Shunammite woman, falling at Elisha's feet wasn't just about humility and submission alone but a desire for the healing and resurrection of her dead son. It was a cry for help. Through her action, the Shunammite woman exemplifies humility and total surrender, mirroring the spiritual act of laying our burdens at the feet of Jesus. It teaches us that true surrender involves acknowledging our helplessness and placing our complete trust in

God's ability to intervene in circumstances that are beyond our control.

And yet at this lowest point in her life, Gehazi is spiritually insensitive and attempts to push her away from the prophet of God, but Elisha intervenes. He recognizes the depth of her distress, highlighting the importance of persistent faith even in the face of rejection from those who ought to show empathy. The action of Gehazi is disappointing, to say the least, the very man who once advocated for the Shunammite woman to have a child pushes her away when she needs him the most!

This serves as a humbling reminder that sometimes people do not always act the way we expect them to. The Shunammite woman never expected the prophet's servant to turn into an obstacle! However, her determination did not waver and her story encourages us to persist in our faith and prayers, even when we encounter resistance or feel overlooked. We have been given full access into the presence of God through Jesus Christ; never allow anyone to deny you what is rightfully yours.

Hidden pain is the most devastating pain because there is a realization that unless God reveals it to you, there is nothing to go by. Elisha realized that the Lord had hidden the Shunammite woman's distress from him as a reminder that he too was human and needed to lean on God for answers. The truth is that, sometimes, even spiritual leaders may not immediately perceive the depth of our pain and struggles. It is crucial to openly express our pain and needs to God and those He places in our lives to help us.

This is not the time to test the validity of one's office or anointing but to be vulnerable and honest. It is a wake-up call and a strong reminder for spiritual leaders that we should all remain sensitive, empathetic, and attuned to the unspoken needs of those we serve. Elisha's acknowledging that the Lord had hidden her distress from him teaches us the concept of spiritual sensitivity and divine timing. Sometimes, God allows us to experience certain situations without immediate clarity to strengthen our faith and dependence on Him. This teaches us as leaders to be patient while trusting in God's timing, even when His plans are not immediately revealed. The Scriptures state that we know in part and prophesy in part. There are just times when God will not reveal all to us.

The story of the Shunammite woman reminds us that life's most profound moments of faith often occur at the feet of the Master. Whether we are experiencing joy or sorrow, success or failure, the posture of humility and surrender is where we find our true strength. The principles derived from the Shunammite woman's story can be applied to various aspects of our modern lives. Whether in personal, professional, or spiritual contexts, living purposefully is crucial all because of her decision to saddle the donkey and embark on a journey to seek Elisha. We must move intentionally in all that we do. Either good, bad or otherwise, it must be laced with a sense of urgency and purpose.

We should reflect on how unexpected challenges are bound to come to test our faith and strengthen the areas of our empathetic leadership and persistence. We must learn the lessons of hidden pain, humility, persistent faith, divine timing, and unwavering faith. As we pilot our own lives, let us embrace the call to live purposefully, saddle up with intention, and lead with clarity. By doing so, we open ourselves to the possibility of extraordinary outcomes and the fulfillment of our greatest potential.

Finally, let us continually seek to place ourselves at the Master's feet knowing that it is there we will find the grace, strength, and answers we need to navigate the journey of life.

CHAPTER SIX
IT IS WELL!

It Is Well!

23 And he said, "Why will you go to him today? It is neither a new moon nor Sabbath." She said, "All is well."

2 KINGS 4:23

IT IS WELL!

It is well! Three simple words with great significance in which amid great pain the Shunammite woman chose to respond differently. Her faith was truly remarkable. Despite facing the heartbreaking death of her only son, she chooses to speak words of faith rather than despair. When her husband questions her sudden decision to seek the prophet Elisha, she reassures him with, "All is well," indicating her steadfast belief in God's power to bring life and restoration. It will eventually serve as a testament to her unwavering faith. Faith is the key to pleasing God, as stated in Hebrews 11:6, and it is impossible to please Him without it!

> *But without faith it is impossible to [walk with God and] please Him, for whoever comes [near] to God must [necessarily] believe that God exists and that He rewards those who [earnestly and diligently seek Him.*
>
> **HEBREWS 11:6 (AMP)**

This verse is the cornerstone of this chapter, which centers on our faith; it also underscores the fundamental importance of our faith relationship with God. Without it, we are not only disconnected from Him but we cannot gain His favor either. Equipped with our faith, we have the power to change the outcome of our lives. By it we can shape our perceptions, actions, and ultimately our destiny. We are a product of the faith we declare; by speaking words of faith and trust in God's promises, we set in motion the divine transformative power that can change our circumstances.

For the Shunammite woman, "All is well" was not a denial of her reality but a declaration of her faith in God's sovereignty. She understood that her circumstances, no matter how dire, were under God's control. Her statement reflected her trust in God's ability to work miracles and her refusal to succumb to impossibility. This is why her story is a powerful example of how faith can alter the course of events and bring about miraculous outcomes.

In essence, faith is not just a passive belief but an active declaration and trust in God's goodness and faithfulness. It empowers us to rise above our challenges and see the possibilities beyond our current struggles. When we respond to life's difficulties with faith, we align ourselves with God's will and open the door to His blessings and miracles. The Shunammite woman had a reference point to start with. She had witnessed firsthand how God had transformed her story of childlessness many years earlier. Her personal experience of God's miraculous intervention served as a powerful reminder of His faithfulness and capability.

It is because of this reference point; that she was convinced that God would not disappoint her in her time of need. Her previous experience with God's faithfulness was not just a distant memory but a living testament to His power and love. It provided a solid foundation for her current faith. She knew that the same God who had given her a child when it seemed impossible was more than capable of restoring life to her son. Her calm response amidst chaos demonstrates incredible inner strength along with her faith, allowing her to see beyond her immediate grief, focusing on the possibility of divine intervention.

Many years ago, during prayer, God revealed to me that *"Faith is living in the reality that what I am believing in God for has already been made available to me."* This revelation gave me a profound understanding of how faith shapes our perception and our responses to life's challenges! It allowed me to fully engage in God's assignment, trusting that the necessary resources have been provided, even when I can't see them. If the Shunammite woman shared a similar perspective, how could she respond otherwise? Suddenly, her faith enhanced her perspective, which would produce her strength! All stemming from a place of unwavering belief that God would act on her behalf.

When you break down Hebrews 11, it becomes about the Principle of Faith, believing that what we hope for is already ours. This in turn transforms how we face and approach life's difficulties. It adjusts our mindset from doubt and despair to confidence, expectation, and anticipation! Thus, the Shunammite woman's faith wasn't a wish but an active trust in the totality of God's promises. She lived in the reality of God's provision, even before she saw the manifestation of His miracle. Now that is FAITH!

Her story illustrates that faith isn't merely hoping for a positive outcome but living as though the desired outcome is already in existence. This kind of faith pleases God while activating His power in our lives. It provokes us to respond to our trials and tribulations with deep-seated confidence in God's unchanging nature and His commitment to fulfilling His promises. With her faith deeply rooted in her past experiences in God and His assurances, her strong foundation enabled her to face her crisis with a resolute and unwavering trust in God's ability to bring life out of death, hope out of despair, and joy out of sorrow.

Your faith gives God the spiritual and legal right to operate in your life, serving as a ticket to access the supernatural realm, where God's power and miracles can manifest—in contrast to unbelief and doubt, which place you in a state of spiritual darkness and blindness, cutting one off from the flow of divine intervention. The enemy, who is fully aware of the power of faith, constantly targets the belief system of Christians. If the devil can sow seeds of doubt while getting you to believe contrary to God's promises, he gains a foothold in your life.

Everything begins in the mind, the constant battleground for all believers. This is why it is crucial to continually feed on the Word of God to establish and maintain personal victory. The greatest battle I have fought as a believer has always centered on my faith. Whenever God assigns me a major task, my faith comes under intense attack. I find myself grappling with fear and doubt, wondering how the task will be accomplished, where the provision will come from, and if God will show up at all.

Faith is our lifeline; it is essential for navigating life's challenges while fulfilling God's purposes. To cultivate one's faith requires daily immersion of oneself in the Word of God. One should also engage in a consistent prayer life while exercising endurance. Faith never gives up, even in the face of overwhelming odds; it's a resilient force that grows stronger through trials and adversities.

Here are four main ways to strengthen your faith: -

1. **Engage the Word of God:** Regular reading and meditating on the scripture leads to building a solid foundation by renewing your mind and fortifying your belief system against the enemy's lies.

2. **Engage in Prayer:** Consistent prayer is crucial in maintaining a close relationship with God. It's through prayer that you receive divine guidance, strength, and reassurance that God is in control. Prayer must be word-based. Praying with the Word of God makes prayer effective and result-yielding.

3. **Exercising Endurance:** Faith requires patience and perseverance. Endurance enables you to stand firm and wait for God's timing, even when immediate answers or solutions are not apparent.

4. **Strengthening Faith through Trials:** Challenges and difficulties are opportunities for your faith to be tested and refined. Each victory over a trial strengthens your faith, making it more robust and resilient.

To build the Shunammite woman's kind of faith we must show the importance of positive declaration; speaking words of faith, hope, and affirmation can transform our mindset. By doing so we align our thoughts with God's promises rather than our fears. It builds encouragement to declare God's goodness even in times when we fail to see the immediate evidence of it.

Life's challenges can be overwhelming, but maintaining a posture of faith and hope enables us to navigate through adversity with hidden strength. The Shunammite woman's example encourages us as Christians to remain resilient, knowing that God is our ever-present help. We learn to hold on to hope in dire circumstances by our confessions. Our hope should be anchored in God's unchanging nature and His promises while we take decisive steps of faith. Our faith walk requires faith in action as well, moving forward by the Word of God or by God's prompting.

Let us remember that faith is not a passive attribute but an active force that requires continuous nurturing. This is especially important when you are faced with daunting assignments from God. Hold on to your faith. You must remember that He who has called you is faithful and will provide all that you need. Your faith is your most powerful weapon in the spiritual battle and, with it, you can overcome any obstacle and fulfill God's purpose for your life.

SADDLE YOUR HORSE

CHAPTER SEVEN
Hold On! Keep Your Saddle Ready

HOLD ON! KEEP YOUR SADDLE READY

30 But the child's mother said, "As surely as the Lord lives and as you live, I will not leave you." So he got up and followed her.

2 KINGS 4:30

The Shunammite woman's declaration, *"As the Lord lives, and as your soul lives, I will not leave you,"* was made during a moment of intense personal crisis. The miracle child prophesied by Elisha had suddenly died. And so, in her time of deepest distress, she made a resolute decision to seek out Elisha, the man of God who had originally prophesied her late son's birth. Just like the Shunammite woman we must cultivate the habit of holding on to the promises of God, which are 'yes' and 'amen.' We should never rest on our laurels believing that once God has blessed us the devil will leave us alone. Nor should we live in a place of constant fear of losing what God has blessed us with as Job did.

I am certain that the Shunammite woman thought she had everything she wanted in life! She was married, had a home, and great wealth along with connections and social status. And, finally, after many years, she had a child—and a miracle child for that matter. What more could any woman ask for? And suddenly she was robbed or even felt betrayed by the very God and prophet who prophesied her son. When the Shunammite woman approached Elisha, she did so with the heart of a desperate mother. Her words around deception and being led reflected her deep anguish and the gravity of her situation.

How often in life have we resigned ourselves to certain situations and we dare not hope for better and then our dreams come true? But suddenly they are dashed. Maybe it is a big new job or marriage. After years of accepting one's fate, a breakthrough miracle gives us hope for new possibilities only for it to be dashed again. And, suddenly, for many of us, we believe that we are undeserving or it is just another bad thing that has happened to us and we accept it. Not the Shunammite woman! Her son's death seemed to negate the promise of God, leaving her feeling betrayed and heartbroken. Yet, even in her despair, she sought out the man of God, and that speaks volumes about her faith and the lessons we can take from her actions.

She confronted Elisha; when was the last time you confronted a man or woman of God who prophesied an opportunity and failed afterwards? What was your posture of faith? Did you walk away leaving that thing dead or did you persist to the very end? The Shunammite woman didn't hide her emotions or sugarcoat her pain. Instead, she took her raw, unfiltered feelings to the prophet. Christians must understand that God can handle our honesty and that our genuine cries for help are heard and valued by Him. Psalm 56:8 speaks about our pain and cries.

> *You keep track of all my sorrows. You have collected all my tears in your bottle. You have recorded each one in your book.*
>
> **PSALM 56:8 (NLT)**

God has a record of our tears and He is moved by every single one of them. While Elisha goes on to instruct Gehazi, my focus is still on the interaction between Elisha and the Shunammite woman. While Elisha responded to her plea by sending his servant with his staff, a symbol of power and authority, it did nothing to comfort the Shunammite woman. This is important for two reasons; firstly, the word did not come through Gehazi but by Elisha. While there are incidents in the Bible in which intermediaries or third parties have acted in the stead of the primary individual, it would not be enough in this case. It was Elisha or no one at all!

Secondly, she was going to hold on to the man of God as a sign of not only holding on to God but also to the promises that were made to her. We too must cultivate the same type of dogmatic behavior if we are to revive our dead miracles! There are certain things that we will never resurrect if we have the attitude "what is for me is for me and what isn't is not." What if the devil does not want you to have that miracle? Will you just walk away or will you fight for it tooth and nail like the Shunammite woman?

The Shunammite woman simply refused to leave Elisha alone. Despite what seemingly looked like a hopeless situation, she clung to Elisha, the man of God, as her only hope. She had no plan B, she was all in, just like Jacob who struggled with the angel of the Lord. Both individuals felt a sense of hopelessness and despair and both of them decided that they would not let go until they got what they came for! The Shunammite woman's resolve teaches us the importance of holding on to our faith, especially during times of crisis.

The Shunammite woman was persistent, even when her situation seemed beyond repair; she refused to accept defeat. The tenacity of modern-day believers to persist in prayer and faith, even when circumstances seem insurmountable, must rise to the level of the Shunammite woman! If we remain in a place of comfort and ease, we will not get all the promises God has prepared for us. God honors persistent faith, and breakthrough often comes to those who refuse to let go. How else can we put on display God's sovereignty and power, even in death, if we fail to persist by actively seeking God's intervention?

I admire the Shunammite woman's unyielding resolve as she was determined to stay with Elisha until her situation was addressed. We must be determined and our faith must be unwavering to get the miracles. We all must continue seeking God's presence even when there are seemingly insurmountable obstacles before us. The action of the Shunammite woman holding on to Elisha was out of desperation and recognition of his spiritual authority. For her, Elisha represented both God's power and His presence on earth. Her act of grasping Elisha tightly symbolizes us clinging to God's promises and His representatives in our lives.

We are not to worship his representatives or put them on a pedestal or place God with them, but we are to access them as they pertain to those areas of blessings that God has promised us. As believers, we shouldn't give up, even when answers are delayed or the situation seems completely hopeless.

The Shunammite woman's insistence that Elisha must follow her speaks to the need for believers to seek help from godly leaders within the Christian faith when facing insurmountable challenges. Take your time and connect with a leader who is grounded in the Word of God. It is also important to build relationships that one can lean on in times of trouble.

My prayer for you is that God will connect you to leaders after His own heart who will create a safe space for you in times of trouble or distress.

Faith must be in active pursuit of something or someone and the Shunammite woman's journey to find Elisha and her refusal to leave without him cements the fact that real faith requires both action and tenacity. As Christians we must act on our faith, seeking God's will and direction through prayer, fasting, and engaging our community along with our faith leaders. We must understand that in times of crisis, we have to persist in prayer while staying encouraged even amid delays and tribulations.

We must keep our focus on God's promises while pressing forward, leaning on God until our breakthrough comes. We should not allow the devil to isolate us from our church community. This will allow us to collaborate and also raise intercession for those who need support and spiritual reinforcement in tough times.

When we all work together, we are reminded of God's promises and when we actively seek God's face as a single unit, it helps galvanize our efforts towards achieving spiritual breakthroughs for all. Faith must have action tied to it, we cannot just pray while sitting down and doing nothing. Faith must be demonstrated through actions just as the Shunammite woman faced many challenges to find Elisha and refused to leave him until he helped her. As Christians we should be proactive in our faith journey, taking steps that may sometimes be considered challenging and align with our prayers and beliefs.

The Shunammite woman's declaration, "I will not leave you," is a powerful testament to her strength of faith, tenacity, perseverance, the role of spiritual leadership, and refusal to take no for an answer. For modern Christians, this is a wake-up call not to leave your miracle lying dead on the ground but to persistently seek God and engage trustworthy spiritual leaders who are willing to stand with you until you get your breakthrough. Know that, through faith and persistence, breakthroughs are possible and God's promises are sure.

CONCLUSION

Dear reader,

In the conclusion of *Saddle Your Horse*, it is essential to reflect on the powerful lessons drawn from the story of the Shunammite woman and her son. We have journeyed together throughout this book exploring faith, resilience, worship, active faith, and determination and we have arrived safely at the ultimate lesson: This final chapter will delve into three specific areas:

1. What it truly means to stay prepared
2. How to live a life of readiness
3. How to respond to life's challenges with grace and strength

Before we get into the specifics, let me assure you that God always stages us for breakthroughs. Regardless of what the enemy has done, you are destined to triumph. God's plans for your life are far greater than any obstacles you face. He turns every setback into a setup for a greater comeback. Remember, every challenge is an opportunity for God to demonstrate His power and faithfulness in your life. Stay rooted in His promises, for He is the one who turns

CONCLUSION

your mourning into joy and your trials into testimonies. Trust in His timing and know that your victory is already secured.

1. The Journey of Preparation of the Shunammite Woman

The Shunammite woman's story reflects the story of all our lives at one point or another. The truth is life is a journey that comes with unexpected twists and turns which are often unplanned and unscheduled. The story of the Shunammite woman and her dead son is a poignant reminder that unexpected challenges can strike at any moment. And the lesson for every modern-day Christian is to be prepared for life's uncertainties.

We must unlearn the Christian myth that once saved we will have no problems. This is wrong as our faith is not a guarantee of a trouble-free life, but it equips us to handle crises with grace and resilience. Prepare like the five wise virgins who had extra oil for a late bridegroom. Prepare for the rainy days of life. Prepare enough for the unexpected to happen, prepare to the best of your ability.

Another lesson in staying prepared is to take a moment for yourself. Take a walk or a break—do whatever you need to do before making a major decision. Clear your head, pray, and then move without hesitation. Self-doubt is a faith-killer, do not entertain any such thoughts even if you are unsure on the inside. Be ready to walk alone as sometimes friends, family, or even your spouse might not be able to help you.

A third lesson is about the power of privacy and remaining focused amid a crisis. When the Shunammite woman's son died, she laid him on Elisha's bed and shut the door, creating a sacred space for a miracle. This single act symbolizes the need for Christians to shut out distractions and negative influences when seeking God's intervention. In today's world, where distractions abound, the lesson is clear: find a quiet place to pray, reflect, and seek God's presence before making any decision. Having a strong prayer life helps you stay prepared to overcome any challenge.

Shutting the door signifies a deliberate act of faith to create an environment where God can work miracles. It reminds us that some battles are won in the secret place of the Most High away from the public eye. When we dwell in the secret place, He becomes our refuge and we know we can trust in Him when we need Him the most. The Shunammite woman must have been introduced to the God of the secret place, the one who answers in quietness where there are no distractions.

CONCLUSION

The fourth lesson is about taking deliberate action, which she did immediately. When her son fell ill and died, she did not succumb to despair or depression; instead, she had a brief conversation with her husband, saddled her donkey, and took decisive action by seeking out Elisha, the man of God. Some critical decisions in life need a quick response; quick thinking on one's toes is important. Her action was a declaration of her intent to seek help and her refusal to accept her situation as final.

Finally, despite the emotional toll of her son's death, she maintained her composure and focus. Her resilience allowed her to push through the pain and take decisive action. Her faith in God and in Elisha's ability to intercede on her behalf was unshaken; her belief in miracles led her to act on that belief. Everything she did in life prepared her for such a moment as this in which her faith would be tested and how she respond matter the most.

2. THE LIFE-CHANGING LESSONS OF READINESS

The Shunammite woman's story teaches us that readiness is about being prepared, not just for the expected but also for the unexpected. Life is unpredictable and challenges can arise without warning. Keeping your saddle ready means living a life of preparedness and resilience. It also means stepping out of our comfort zone, doing things we have never done before, and pushing ourselves in ways that we ordinarily would never do. A state of readiness is a state that requires you to pivot sometimes in the opposite direction of your emotions, and your feelings while testing your faith. There are several life-changing lessons of readiness that every believer should best be equipped to handle.

- **Spiritual Readiness:** Maintaining a strong spiritual foundation, just as the Shunammite woman's faith was the cornerstone of her readiness. Nurture your faith through prayer, study the Word of God, and build a close relationship with Him.

- **Emotional Readiness:** Build emotional resilience. Life will test us, but having the emotional strength to face challenges head-on is crucial. Practice self-care and seek support when needed along with staying grounded.

- **Practical Readiness:** Do not only be spiritually prepared but practically as well. Do not be the type of Christian who is heavenly prepared but earthly unequipped. This means we must have a plan in place including a contingency plan as well. We must also be organized and stay informed about what is happening around us; this means being up to date on the current situation.

- **Act Outside the Box:** May we all find the courage to break protocol in moments of great desperation and faith. The Shunammite woman's determination to defy social and religious norms to seek a miracle changed the outcome of her situation. Modern-day Christians must learn the important lesson that persistent faith and some breakthroughs will require us to step outside of conventional boundaries and norms.

The Shunammite woman's sense of urgency and consistency shows us that desperate times call for desperate measures. Her actions encourage us to sometimes break free of tradition or societal expectations when seeking God's intervention.

- **Understand Purpose:** Adversity has a way of making us rediscover who we are. Adversity will teach you a few things and reveal the strength you never knew you had. It will test your resolve, challenge your faith, and ultimately shape you into a more resilient and purposeful individual. Through trials, you gain clarity on what truly matters and you emerge with a deeper understanding of your life's purpose and a stronger connection to the path God has set before you. The Shunammite woman's purposeful actions were driven by her deep faith and determination to see her son restored and uncovered a hidden strength and drive that she never knew she was capable of and this made all the difference, cementing her miracle! Her purpose guided her decision, which was to save her son. Let your purpose be a beacon that directs your steps.

- **Saddle Purposefully and Be Ready for Anything:** Once your purpose is clear and your actions are determined, it's time to act without hesitation. Do not allow room for fear or doubt but move forward with confidence; sometimes it might be just a little, but still move. If your actions align with your purpose, then you are heading in the right direction. Embrace the unexpected in the journey of life as life is full of surprises, both good and bad. Keeping your saddle ready means being adaptable and open to what you may have to experience along the way.

- **Cultivate the Spirit of Flexibility:** I have met people who boast about being inflexible and I often feel a great sense of loss for them. A willingness to adapt demonstrates several key qualities

CONCLUSION

as people. Adaptability showcases our resilience and how quickly we can recover from difficulties. In the face of unexpected challenges, our ability to adapt and find new solutions demonstrates our mental and emotional strength. It also brings into play how we can adjust our plans in response to changing circumstances. This is crucial in crises where the original course of action may no longer be viable and we now need to be resourceful as well. Creative thinking and problem-solving skills are enhanced under pressure.

Flexibility means that we are open-minded with the emotional intelligence to manage our emotions in times when we want to react. There is something about flexibility that ties to our ability to be empathetic, all the while using such experiences as teachable moments of courage and growth. It takes bravery to abandon familiar paths and venture into the unknown, trusting in our ability to handle whatever comes next. The Shunammite woman did not know what to expect when she reached Prophet Elisha, but she was ready to adapt to whatever situation she found herself in.

3. RESPOND TO LIFE'S CHALLENGES WITH GRACE AND STRENGTH

Finally, the Shunammite woman's story is one about handling pressure under grace while at the same time exhibiting strength. This is not often the case as many people tend to bend under the pressures of life. Our response to life's challenges can often determine whether we get a favorable outcome or not. There were many instances when the Shunammite woman could have acted according to her situation, but she did not. She showed incredible leadership skills under unspeakable pressure. We must learn the power to do the same.

- **Openness to Change:** When we accept that life is a journey, we begin to move as people who understand this concept. If you have ever traveled, you will learn that some of your most memorable trips were riddled with challenges from a delayed flight to a fully booked hotel you had made reservations for several months in advance! While these are inconvenient moments, they often require us to be open to change, leading to an opportunity for growth. Life's challenges can be a catalyst for transformation and new beginnings, often leading to a better version of ourselves.

- **Staying Grounded While Never Giving Up:** One of the Shunammite woman's most powerful show of grace was her refusal to let prophet Elisha go. She was not rude or disrespectful, but in quiet and gentle defiance she maintained her resolve concerning him. This was truly graceful under pressure. She did not give up; all the while she remained grounded and consistent. Know that during life's storms, staying grounded is essential and the Shunammite woman's composure and focus are a reminder of the importance of being positioned.

- **Trusting the Process:** In God's perfect timing, He makes all things beautiful. It's essential to allow God to work in His own time, resisting the urge to rush the process. We must remain confident that He knows what is best for us. Even when protocols are broken, there is often a process that follows. Trusting the process also involves embracing the journey, even when the outcome is uncertain. True faith in action means moving forward with trust and confidence, even when the path is unclear. A key part of this trust is understanding that our role in the process involves actively engaging our faith. Faith without action is incomplete, so we must do our part, trusting that God will do His.

This trust is not passive but active, requiring us to lean into the journey, taking each step with the assurance that God's timing is perfect and His plans are for our good. Even in moments of doubt or uncertainty, we can rest in the knowledge that He is in control and will guide us to the fulfillment of His promises.

The Shunammite woman's story exemplifies how faith, when combined with decisive actions, can lead to miraculous outcomes. For modern-day Christians, trusting the process is seen through our daily walks, whether it is prayer, worship, or service. It's about having a clear vision and mission, and knowing that the process is working for our good. We must understand that at the Master's feet, total surrender and trust are required with us laying our burdens before him.

- **Positive Affirmation and Inner Peace:** The declaration "It is well" by the Shunammite woman, even in the face of her son's death, is a profound statement of faith but also a form of affirmation. Today's Christians must cultivate the habit of positive confession, which holds the power to change our

CONCLUSION

bad situation for the better. When we confess the positive, it shifts our perspectives by increasing our faith, hence altering how we view our circumstances. This is the way we can build up our inner peace that often leads to meditation, prayer, and self-reflection.

- **Staying Focused While Growing:** Do not let distractions or setbacks derail you from your path. There will be obstacles and disappointments along the way, but that is part of the journey process. Stay committed to yourself and what you want to achieve. Also, commit to continuous self-growth and learning. Many times, people lose the essential lessons that each problem brings and the benefits that emerge from them. Know that each challenge is an opportunity to personally learn and grow from it. It is also a place where you discover your niche as well as your next life purpose.

- **The Role of Community and Support:** While there will be lonely points in this journey called life, we are not meant to take it alone. The Shunammite woman was alone twice, when her son was in her arms and when he died. Even on her trip to the prophet she had her servant. While seeking out Prophet Elisha, the Shunammite woman recognized the power of community and the importance of seeking help from others. Don't remain in isolation; please do not hesitate to seek support from others. Whether it's friends, family, or mentors, having a good support system can provide the strength and encouragement that is needed.

- **Building All Types of Relationships:** Relationship is currency. While strategic relationships are vital, it is equally important to build various strong and supportive relationships as well. The bonds you create can be a source of support in times of need and challenges. Learn to invest in the right relationships that provide benefits in times of trouble.

The restorative power of God is truly beautiful. While scars may remain, they serve as reminders of our journey—testimonies of what God has done in our lives. Each mark tells a story, not just of pain, but of healing, growth, and unwavering grace. These reminders invite us to reflect on the transformative moments when God's love shone through our darkest times. Embrace the beauty of restoration; it is through our scars that we witness the profound depth of His mercy and the hope that lies ahead. God is the restorer of soul and I have seen Him do mighty miracles in so many people's lives. Do not circumvent the process but work through it with Him. And just like in the case of Job, He will give you double for your trouble! He has His ways and how He will choose to bring your restoration is totally up to Him. I have learned over the years not to interrupt the process by pulling my own cards or overthinking how He will get it done.

Let us surrender to Him as the Shunammite woman did; if we say we have submitted to His will, then let us allow Him to take over all of it. Lay down all your cards and let Him have His way. Refuse to get in the way and stop telling Him how you think it should be done. How can the pot tell the potter what is best for it? The story of the Shunammite woman has been a favorite of mine for years. Her tenacity and strength often inspire me. She serves as a powerful reminder of the importance of readiness, faith, and purposeful action.

As you move forward in life, keep your saddle ready. Be prepared for the unexpected, respond with purpose, persist through challenges, and stay grounded in your faith. By doing so, you will be equipped to handle whatever comes your way and transform challenges into triumphs. I hope that you too will come to love the story of the Shunammite woman and through the words of this book, you will equally learn a few things from her.

More importantly, may you receive strength in this very moment to rise out of whatever pain you find yourself. I pray that the Lord Jesus will touch you and pull you out. It's never too late and you are not a failure. You can do it; His strength is made perfect in your weakness.

By His Grace
Marian (E.M.)

THANK YOU

To my new family of readers, I want to sincerely thank you for grabbing a copy of this book. My hope and prayer for you is that, as you have finished reading Saddle Your Horse, you have discovered your inner strength to face life's challenges. May the grace of God and the reviving spirit of the LORD stir you up and restore you speedily.

E.M.

SALVATION PRAYER

Perhaps you have read this book today and have realized that you are not where you are supposed to be in your relationship with Jesus Christ or you may have even backslidden. Here is an opportunity to say the sinner's prayer to get things right with Him and begin to end the pattern of dysfunction in your life.

Heavenly Father, today I invite you into my life to commit my will, my spirit, and my soul over to you. I acknowledge that I am a sinner and I am sorry for the sins that I have committed in the past and request your forgiveness.

I confess Jesus Christ as my personal Lord and Savior. I believe in your only begotten son Jesus Christ and that by the shedding of His blood at the Cross of Calvary my sins have been washed away and I stand as a new creature in Christ Jesus because I have fully believed. I believe in the baptism, death, and resurrection of Jesus Christ and that my life is hidden in Christ and I am now saved.

I now thank Jesus for His undying love and grace at the Cross and that I have access to the throne of grace in times of trouble and tribulation. I also accept the Holy Spirit as the guide and teacher of my life through this new and wonderful journey of abundant life. Lord, transform my life and mold me into what you want me to be now that I am saved. Amen.

www.ingramcontent.com/pod-product-compliance
Lightning Source LLC
LaVergne TN
LVHW011425080426
835512LV00005B/279